THE
OFFICIAL
guide to accompanying learner drivers

London: The Stationery Office

Published by The Stationery Office for the Driving Standards Agency under licence from the Controller of Her Majesty's Stationery Office.

© Crown Copyright 2000

Applications for reproduction should be made in writing to
The Copyright Unit, Her Majesty's Stationery Office,
St Clements House, 2–16 Colegate, Norwich NR3 1BQ

ISBN 0 11 552178 X

A CIP catalogue record for this book is available from the British Library

Other titles in the Official Driving Series

The Official Theory Test for Car Drivers and Motorcyclists

The Official Theory Test for Drivers of Large Vehicles

The Official Driving Test

The Official Driving Manual

The Official Bus and Coach Driving Manual

The Official Goods Vehicle Driving Manual

The Official Compulsory Basic Training for Motorcyclists

The Official Motorcycling Manual

The Official Tractor and Specialist Vehicle Driving Tests

The Official DSA Guide for Driving Instructors

The Official Theory Test CD-ROM – 'Your Licence to Drive'

Acknowledgments

The Driving Standards Agency (DSA) would like to thank the staff of The Department of the Environment, Transport and the Regions for their contribution to the production of this publication

Every effort has been made to ensure that the information contained in this publication is accurate at the time of going to press. The Stationery Office cannot be held responsible for any inaccuracies. Information in this book is for guidance only.

The Driving Standards Agency (DSA) is an executive agency of the Department of the Environment, Transport and the Regions.

You'll see its logo at test centres.

The aim of DSA is to promote road safety through the advancement of driving standards.

DSA

- conducts practical driving tests for drivers or riders of cars, mopeds, motorcycles, lorries, buses and other vehicles
- plans, maintains and supervises the theory test for drivers or riders of cars, mopeds, motorcycles, lorries and buses
- controls the register of Approved Driving Instructors (ADIs)
- controls the voluntary register of Large Goods Vehicle (LGV) instructors
- supervises Compulsory Basic Training (CBT) courses for motorcyclists
- aims to provide a high-quality service to its customers.

DSA Website

www.driving-tests.co.uk

CONTENTS

CONTENTS

First the bad news

On average, ten people die every day on the UK's roads and hundreds more are seriously injured.

Newly qualified drivers account for far more than their fair share of these accidents. Check the insurance premiums of a new driver against those of an experienced driver. That will give an idea of how big a risk new drivers are known to be.

Now for the good news

Statistics show that the risk to newly qualified drivers decreases with miles driven and experience gained. If that experience is gained before the driving test is passed then the likelihood of an accident in those first few critical months can be reduced.

The key to it all is practice. Driving a motor car is a complex business that takes much longer to master than most people appreciate. Rushing to take the driving test before enough experience has been gained is a mistake. About half the people who present themselves for their practical driving test haven't mastered basic driving skills. However, those who have had plenty of practice on a variety of roads, and at different times of the day and night, are more likely to pass their driving test at the first attempt and go on to have a reduced risk of accident in their early years of driving unaccompanied.

Driving is a complex and exciting activity but one not to be taken lightly. To almost ten people every day in the UK it is also a fatal activity. Getting enough practice of the right type before passing the driving test is a big step towards achieving 'Safe driving for life'.

Robin Cummins

The Chief Driving Examiner
Driving Standards Agency

This book is aimed at those experienced drivers who want to help a learner driver gain driving experience through practice.

It's not a driving instruction manual but a guide to help with questions such as 'When?', 'Where?' and 'How much?' while offering guidance to help steer around some of the pitfalls and problems that may arise. Being a passenger in your own car with a learner driving can be an unsettling experience. Keeping in mind your reason for being there should help; and take comfort from the fact that accidents while learning are very rare indeed.

Books to help

It is strongly recommended that you have a copy of *The Highway Code* (The Stationery Office) handy for reference. You can buy one from any good bookshop.

The DSA Official series of books provide a good source of knowledge of driving skills and safe practices.

The Official Theory Test for Car Drivers and Motorcyclists, *The Official Driving Test*, *The Official Driving Manual* and *Know Your Traffic Signs* are also published by The Stationery Office.

The Official Theory Test and Beyond (The Stationery Office) is a CD-ROM providing a fun and modern way of learning the theory of driving safely.

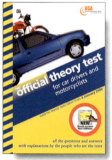

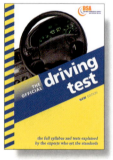

To learn how to drive, the Driving Standards Agency recommends a combination of formal tuition and private practice. Formal driving tuition can **only** be given by either a trainee or a qualified Approved Driving Instructor (ADI) (see p. 53) who can also help structure the private practice. Look on the process of making your relative or friend a safe driver as a team effort involving you, your learner and their ADI. Working together is the best way of ensuring everyone's aim of safe driving for life.

The ADI may already have issued your learner with a Driver's Logbook. It's not compulsory to have a logbook but it can be very helpful for

- learners to keep track of their progress
- letting your learner know the topics to practise
- letting the ADI know how you and your learner have got on.

Part Four of this book contains a copy of the Driver's Logbook

If you feel unsure about anything or want a bit of advice, you can talk to the ADI about the areas which concern you. You may want to accompany your learner on their next lesson to see how the ADI copes with situations you find difficult. Make sure your learner is happy for you to sit in on their lesson and arrange a suitable time with the ADI.

Sometimes you may think the ADI is teaching a driving technique which seems wrong to you. Remember, as cars become more sophisticated, so recommended techniques change to take advantage of new technology. The ADI is probably using the most up-to-date methods which may be different to the way you were taught. Don't confuse your learner by expecting them to do things 'your way'. One part of your role is to enable your learner to practise the techniques taught by their ADI.

Agreeing to accompany a learner driver is a responsibility not to be taken lightly. When you accompany a learner driver you're responsible for their actions and your licence is at risk if you allow motoring offences to be committed.

This part of the book introduces you to the task of being an accompanying driver and will give you some idea of what you may expect.

The topics covered

- Beginning
- Training
- Where you fit in
- Can you do it legally?
- What can you expect?
- Personal qualities
- The practice vehicle
- Conflicts
- When to start
- Early days
- Planning.

Beginning

For a new driver there's an awful lot to learn. The list includes

- the theory
- learning how to operate a complicated set of controls (which looks so easy)
- operating the controls while putting the theory into practice
- judgement
- anticipation and awareness.

As well as coping with

- other road users
- the weather
- road conditions
- navigation.

Even after basic control skills have developed, being able to cope with constantly changing demands and unexpected events – often in a fraction of a second – are skills which come with experience. The whole business is complicated, challenging and, for some, extremely difficult. To expect that all this can be learned in a few short lessons is a mistake.

Did you know?

New drivers cannot begin driving until they have received their licence from Swansea and it has come into effect.

A learner driver needs to gain enough skill and experience to enable them to drive alone safely once they have passed their driving test. As more miles are driven and more experience is gained, the novice driver will gradually progress towards becoming an experienced driver. However, driving is a subject where there are always new lessons to be learned and it is a foolish and dangerous driver who thinks they know it all.

So how does a learner begin the process of going from novice to competent safe driver?

The answer lies in two key areas

- training – to learn new skills
- practice – to gain experience.

Four Stages of Learning to Drive

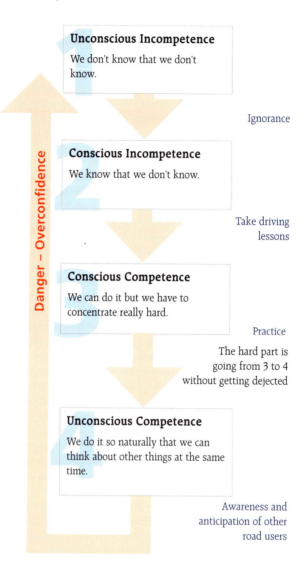

Unconscious Incompetence

We don't know that we don't know.

Ignorance

Conscious Incompetence

We know that we don't know.

Take driving lessons

Conscious Competence

We can do it but we have to concentrate really hard.

Practice

The hard part is going from 3 to 4 without getting dejected

Unconscious Competence

We do it so naturally that we can think about other things at the same time.

Awareness and anticipation of other road users

Danger – Overconfidence

Training

Most people learn to drive with an ADI. Driving instructors are professionals who are trained to teach driving skills in a structured manner to suit differing abilities.

Many pupils only have one or two hours of professional driving instruction each week and their experience is often limited to driving at the same time of day and over the same types of roads.

You need to know

Some insurance companies don't insure people under 25 years of age, or they may offer reduced cover.

Don't risk driving uninsured!

Where you fit in

As an accompanying driver you will be helping your learner have more practice and gain wider experience of the varied driving conditions they are likely to meet once they have passed their driving test.

Know the limits of your driver and don't attempt any driving which will be beyond their ability. Remember, you're helping a new driver to gain skills which will help to keep them safe for many years to come.

Learners who combine extra practice with professional lessons not only perform better on their driving test but go on to have a reduced accident rate in the early years of driving unaccompanied.

That's not to say it will be an easy task and there may be times when you need to remind yourself why you're there.

Can you do it legally?

Before you agree to accompany a learner driver there are a few things you need to check:

Accompanying driver's checklist

Have you held a full EC/EEA driving licence for at least three years for the category of vehicle being driven? . . . . Yes/No

Are you at least 21 years of age? . . . . Yes/No

Is the car you intend to use

- insured for use by the learner? . . . . Yes/No

- fitted with L plates (D plates in Wales) to both the front and rear of the car? . . . . Yes/No

- in a safe roadworthy condition? . . . . Yes/No

The answer must be Yes to *all* questions before you can act as an accompanying driver to a learner.

Did you know?

Only an ADI can charge for driving lessons. Even accepting money for fuel is an offence unless you're an ADI.

Don't be caught out

What can you expect?

To start with, don't expect this to be easy. Learning to drive takes a lot longer than most people realise. You need to set aside plenty of your time for practice sessions so there are no excuses. If you set dates and times when you're expecting to go out with your learner you're more likely to be in a calm frame of mind than if you've had to stop what you were doing and grudgingly give your time.

Be guided by the ADI, but once the basic skills have been learned it's a good idea to let your learner do a lot of the everyday driving, such as to the shops or to school or college.

If your driver struggles with something you think is easy don't worry. Everyone learns at different rates and in different ways and it may be necessary to go over the same ground many times. Memory often plays tricks and you may have forgotten how you struggled with some aspects of learning to drive.

Accident facts

Young drivers are about twice as likely to have an accident negotiating a bend than older drivers.

What are you expecting to achieve?

The goals you should be aiming for are a new driver who

- has practised their new skills until they are both confident and competent
- has a sound basis on which to build their driving career
- has gained enough experience to be able to think for themselves and cope safely with any driving situation
- will be confident about their ability to pass the driving test
- understands their responsibility as a driver.

Personal qualities

Bad habits

It's all too easy for bad habits to creep unnoticed into anyone's driving. Before you act as an accompanying driver it's worth looking at your own driving. You'll have little credibility if you expect your learner to drive one way while you practice another – and don't expect your learner not to notice. Why not have a lesson or two with the ADI yourself? This will allow an expert to check your driving and help you to improve your skills.

Drinking and driving, speed limits, use of signals, seat belts and attitude to other road users are all aspects of driving where standards slip. Setting a good example when you drive will have positive benefits for both you and your learner.

Patience

Frustration can soon set in when your learner struggles with something you think should be easy, or can't do something that they could do the last time you went out. If something is proving difficult, don't keep on until tempers fray. Leave it and come back to it another time. Learning to drive should be an enjoyable experience, not an ordeal.

Other road users may be inconsiderate and show little regard for the fact that your driver is a learner. Don't allow this to wind you up since it will also affect your learner. Knocking a learner driver's confidence can ruin their driving career before it has even started.

Technique

Before accompanying your learner you should give some thought to how you are going to

- give directions
- cope with dangerous situations.

Your learner will need clear directions given calmly and in plenty of time. You will need to look and think that bit further ahead than normal. If your learner has difficulty telling their right from their left you'll need to overcome this problem. Your ADI should be able to give you some advice on these matters, as well as tips on giving directions at any complex junctions in your area.

Safety is your first priority and where possible you should act early and prevent hazards from developing into dangerous situations. If a dangerous situation does develop you may need to

- speak firmly and clearly without shouting
- reach across and take control of the steering wheel
- use the handbrake
- use dual controls if fitted.

Think about this

Learning to drive takes a lot longer than most people think.

Be patient with your learner.

The practice vehicle

Is your car suitable for your learner to drive?

A learner may learn in any make or model of car but a large, powerful car may be more difficult to control than a smaller model. Small cars are not necessarily any easier to drive but their size can make judging the car's position easier, especially during manouevres.

It might be helpful to find a driving school that uses a similar car to your own. If this isn't possible make allowances for your learner if they struggle to adapt to your car after lessons in the school car.

L Plates

Avoid fixing L (D) plates to the windscreen or rear window since they restrict the view. Don't forget to cover or remove the L (D) plates when the car is being used by a full licence holder.

Top tip

Fit an extra rear view mirror. Knowing what's going on behind is important for safety and peace of mind.

Conflicts

Accompanying a novice driver can be frustrating, unnerving and a lot harder than you think.

Here are a few points worth remembering to help you keep on top of it.

- Talking to the ADI will help you plan practice sessions avoiding places which may be too difficult for your learner's present level of ability.

- Learn from mistakes and don't dwell on them. Encouragement and tolerance will help skills and confidence develop.

- Nothing is achieved if you allow yourself to become angry with your learner. If it's all going wrong have a break for five minutes or stop the session altogether if things are too bad.

- If something happens which scares either you or your learner, pull over and give yourselves time to calm down. Discuss what went wrong and why. Were you expecting too much from your learner?

- If another road user fails to show your learner due consideration, don't allow it to upset you. Set a good example, keep calm and turn the experience into a lesson in anticipation.

- Prevent your learner getting into difficulties by looking well ahead and anticipating problems. Don't expect a novice to have the same degree of awareness and judgement as you.

- Your learner is going to drive in the way their instructor has taught. If any techniques differ from the way you drive don't argue over who's right or insist they do it your way. Make a note of what's bothering you and talk about it to the instructor.

Top tip

Keep reminding yourself that you are making a big difference to your learner's long-term driving safety.

Good news!

Learner drivers rarely have crashes while practising.

When to start

DSA recommends that new drivers reach a level of proficiency with an ADI before starting to practise with an accompanying driver. Ask the ADI to tell you when your learner is ready to start practising. Starting too soon may be unnerving for both of you and could lead to anything from a loss of confidence through to a serious loss of control.

Use the Driver's Logbook to see the progress being made and the topics needing practice. To start with this will be mostly control skills but will gradually move on to include the whole syllabus, as set out in the book *The Driving Test* (The Stationery Office).

Early days

Before you begin your first practice sessions you need to give some thought to where and when. Driving in heavy traffic at rush hour isn't going to be good for either of you.

> **Don't forget**
>
> **A learner driver may find driving very tiring.**

Where

Pick a quiet area where

- there won't be much traffic to deal with
- you won't cause a nuisance to other road users or local residents.

It's also a good idea to find somewhere fairly level because of the added difficulties a hill can create at this stage.

Your learner will probably drive quite slowly and, despite your efforts to find somewhere quiet, you may find a queue of traffic building up behind. If this happens, be prepared to ask your learner to pull over somewhere safe and let it pass.

When

Plan the first few practice sessions to avoid busy times of the day. These include

- rush hours
- school start and finish times
- during local events.

Your learner can only practise when you make the time available. Work and other commitments may make demands on you and the only time you have could be evenings and weekends.

In the winter months, evening practice will be in the dark – but don't let this be an excuse not to practise. As long as the weather conditions aren't dangerous, practising in the dark shouldn't be a problem.

> **Many crashes involving young drivers result from lack of experience.**
>
> **Practice builds experience**

Planning

Many learners take their driving lessons at the same time of day and drive repeatedly over the same types of roads. While this may provide a level of familiarity with these roads, it does little to provide a broad experience of the wide variety of driving conditions your learner will meet when they have passed their test.

Good practice sessions should build both experience and confidence. This can be achieved by planning each session around your learner's practice requirements and their driving limitations. To help you with this, refer to their logbook to see which topics need practising.

As part of your planning you will need to think about

- routes
- time of day
- road types
- manoeuvring
- weather conditions.

These are now looked at in turn.

Think about this

Could your learner cope with any situation that might arise?

They will have to when they pass their test.

Routes

Thinking through where you are going to take your learner will enable you to

- avoid areas which may have features such as a steep hill or a difficult junction which they are not yet ready to deal with
- practise certain aspects such as left turns, traffic lights, roundabouts, one way streets, etc.

You don't want to find you have put your learner into a situation which is more than they can cope with and could have been avoided if you had planned ahead.

Time of day

Local knowledge will enable you to know which roads are busiest and when. This will enable you to either

- avoid the worst areas in the early days, or
- practise in busy traffic when your learner is ready.

Daylight, dusk and darkness are all driving conditions which need different skills and need to be practised. Your learner should be able to think independently and use the car's lights when necessary.

Eyesight

If your learner has great difficulty seeing at night get their night vision tested by an optician.

Road types

While a learner cannot use a motorway, they can drive on all other types of road. For example, driving on a dual carriageway calls for skills and techniques that will need to be learned and practised.

If a logbook is being used it will indicate the types of road where practice is needed.

Manoeuvring

The driving test requires manoeuvres to be demonstrated which reflect real driving situations. These include stopping in an emergency, turning the car around in the road, reversing into a side road and parking using reverse gear both on the road and into car park bays.

The ADI will teach the techniques and, if a logbook is being used, will record which have been taught and which need practice.

Think about this

Poor judgement of speed, anticipation and use of controls are key factors in accidents involving inexperienced drivers.

Weather conditions

Many learners begin learning in the spring months and pass the driving test before winter arrives. These learners may have had little or no experience of driving in

- rain
- mist and fog
- windy conditions
- slippery conditions.

These are everyday conditions that most motorists will encounter within their first year of driving. When the ADI indicates your learner is ready to cope with poor weather driving, be prepared to go out in these conditions as they occur.

One word of caution though. Don't underestimate the weather. Extremes of bad weather can make any form of driving unsafe and it is not recommended that you attempt driving practice in severe weather conditions.

If in doubt – don't venture out.

PART TWO LOGBOOK TOPICS

This part refers to the topics listed in the Driver's Logbook (Part Four). When the ADI has indicated areas for practice you can refer to the relevant pages here.

The topics covered

- Vehicle checks
- Ancillary controls
- Starting the engine
- Use of car controls
- Moving off
- Position on the road
- Proper observations
- Turning/emerging left
- Turning/emerging right
- Crossroads
- Roundabouts
- Stationary vehicles
- Safety of others
- Reaction to risk
- Meeting traffic
- Crossing traffic

- Overtaking
- Suitable speed
- Safe distance
- Pedestrian crossings
- Dual carriageways
- Changing lanes
- Signs/markings
- Progress
- Emergency stop
- Turn in the road
- Reversing to the left and right
- Reverse park
- Use of car parks.

Vehicle checks

With today's reliable vehicles it's all too easy to put off vital safety checks and kid ourselves that because everything seems to be going fine we can leave it until some other time.

Do **you** know how often you should be making routine safety checks on your vehicle and what it is you should be checking?

To make sure new drivers have an understanding of the basic safety checks, a 'safety checks' element is included in the official syllabus for learner drivers.

How you can help

Ask your learner to check the car over before each outing. Encourage them to use the owner's manual to find their way around and to find the correct settings. If you have to stop for fuel let your learner refuel the car and while you're there what about letting them check the tyre pressures?

Ancillary controls

To begin with, controlling the steering, gears and foot controls will take all your learner's concentration. As their skill develops it's important for them to become competent with ancillary controls such as demister, wipers, heaters, etc.

How you can help

Allow your learner to familiarise themselves with the layout of the ancillary controls and explain any special features that may be fitted to your car. The ancillary controls may be laid out differently in the ADI's car and this could lead to some confusion, for example, windscreen wiper controls on the left of the steering column or on the right.

Remember your learner should be able to operate these controls without having to look down to find them.

What to expect

When you're in situations which call for the use of ancillary controls, your learner may be concentrating really hard on their driving and fail to realise the need to use them.

Don't allow the situation to become dangerous, such as when the windows are misting up, but do encourage your learner to recognise for themselves when these controls should be used.

If your learner fumbles about trying to find and operate the control they want, pull up somewhere safe and run through the control layout again.

Starting the engine

This may seem almost too easy to you. To a novice the basic checks before starting the engine can appear complicated and remembering everything they need to do can be a struggle.

How you can help

Vehicle manufacturers often supply several keys but only one operates the ignition. Show your learner which key to use and explain how to tell it from the others.

If your vehicle has an alarm, immobiliser or other security device fitted, explain how to use it. You may also need to explain how to release the steering lock to enable the ignition key to turn.

What to expect

Your learner may have been taught a list of checks to make. As they run through their check list make sure the item **is** checked and not just mentioned.

If your vehicle has either a diesel engine or has a modern engine management system, a word of caution. If your learner starts the engine while the car is in gear, the engine management system will try to keep the engine running. If the handbrake isn't set properly this could lead to a dangerous loss of control.

Modern cars can also be so silent and smooth that a learner has difficulty telling whether the engine is running. This can lead to

- keeping the starter key turned after the engine has started
- trying to start an already running engine.

Alert

Don't drop your guard because you're thinking this should be easy – it's not uncommon for learners to find it difficult to tell whether the gear lever really is in neutral before they turn the key.

Use of car controls

This covers the main controls including

- accelerator
- clutch
- gears
- footbrake
- handbrake
- steering.

Many new drivers find that using the controls is one of the most difficult skills to learn. How quickly these skills develop will depend on

- natural ability
- practice.

Skill in using the controls will continue to develop up to the point where they can be used without any conscious effort. Your learner won't be ready to take their driving test until this level has been reached.

How you can help

Your role will be to enable as much practice as possible to take place. Any form of driving will provide practice in use of controls. To begin with, it's a good idea to use quiet roads to reduce the number of other driving hazards your learner will have to cope with.

What to expect

In the early days your learner will be concentrating mainly on how they use the controls and not so much on the other aspects of driving.

Their awareness and judgement may be poor, and the two combined are likely to make this one of the more stressful times for you. If you find it more than you can cope with consider

- telling the ADI how you are feeling. You may need to wait until your learner's control skills are better developed
- accompanying your learner on a lesson with the ADI to see how a professional copes with these difficulties
- fitting dual controls to your car.

Moving off

To move off safely your learner will need

- skill in use of the controls
- sound judgement
- awareness of other road users.

How you can help

To begin with, it's best to practise moving off on a level surface, progressing to sloping surfaces as skill develops.

While your learner is having to concentrate really hard on using the controls, they may forget to watch for other road users. Stay alert and don't let them move off into danger.

Practise moving off

- on the level
- uphill
- downhill
- from behind a parked vehicle.

What to expect

Every time your learner moves off, unless you are in a car with automatic transmission, expect them to go through a lengthy process of finding the biting point and balancing the accelerator and clutch against the handbrake.

This will make moving off a slow process and this in turn makes dealing with road junctions more difficult. At busy junctions you may find frustration sets in as

- traffic builds up behind
- your learner can't pull out into a space which you would find safe as a driver.

If you find your learner has difficulty with busy junctions avoid them until the necessary control skills have developed.

Alert

Traffic lights are one place where tension can build. When the red light changes it's not uncommon for novices to stall the engine in their rush to move off promptly. This can lead to panic, especially if there is a queue of traffic behind. Stay calm and don't react to another driver sounding their horn – they may not be able to see the L plates if they're not immediately behind.

Position on the road

With experience, judging the car's position becomes second nature, but learning to position accurately is a surprisingly difficult skill to learn. This may be due to

- car design which seats the driver on one side of the vehicle
- looking just in front of the car rather than well ahead. This makes it more difficult to judge the car's width and position on the road.

As well as the control skills, your learner will need to know

- where to position for any particular driving situation
- the meaning of signs and road markings.

How you can help

The skill of being able to judge the car's position on the road from the seating position on the right (or left in left-hand drive cars) will develop with practice.

You may need to reach across and steer into the correct position if your learner steers to one side or another. Try to remain calm and don't allow the wrong road position to go uncorrected for any length of time.

In the early days, avoid taking your learner into places where you know accurate judgement is called for, such as a narrow street or roads with width restrictions.

What to expect

Before your learner's judgement has developed you can expect to see

- driving too close to
    - the edge of the road
    - parked cars
    - other obstructions
    - the centre of the road
- poor positioning around bends and junctions
- poor lane discipline.

Some of these mistakes can be quite scary for you in the passenger seat and it's quite likely that your learner will be unaware of both their position error and the way their positioning is making you feel.

If it's going wrong, pull over and talk about any specific problems. Your learner may not think there is anything wrong with the way they have been positioning and you may need to demonstrate their mistake in order for them to see it themselves. If you have a disagreement over where you should position the car, then refer it to the ADI.

Alert

Don't allow your learner to hit the kerb while driving normally. The impact may wrench the steering wheel from their grasp causing serious loss of control. Alternatively it may damage or burst the tyre.

Proper observations

Your learner will have to learn where and when they should be looking, and what it is they are looking for. Interpreting what they see and planning how to deal with the possible outcomes is a skill which develops with experience.

The Driver's Logbook breaks this topic down into

- blind spots
- forward observations
- use of mirrors.

How you can help

Blind spots   There are blind spots on all cars but some are worse than others. You can help by removing any unnecessary stickers, ornaments or mascots which might obstruct the view or cause a distraction.

Even if your learner checks their blind spots when they should, you'll still have to look yourself since their judgement may be poor and they could be driving into danger.

Forward observations   When accompanying your learner you will need to look well ahead to pick out potential hazards in good time. However, as your learner becomes more experienced avoid prompting them too soon. This may lead to a dependence on your prompt and a reduced ability to think for themselves.

Use of mirrors   The ADI will teach the use of mirrors early on in the training process. To check if your learner is using their mirrors correctly, fit another small interior mirror, angled so that you can see your learner without having to look directly at them.

What to expect

Blind spots Despite your learner going through the motions of checking their blind spots, there will be occasions when they see a hazard but either don't recognise it or don't know how to react. Stay one step ahead and be ready to help as soon as you're needed.

Forward observation New drivers often don't look very far ahead and

- are slow to identify potential danger
- don't realise how soon they need to react.

Step in to help before any danger develops.

Use of mirrors Most drivers learn to use the mirror quite quickly. If your learner is missing mirror checks you will need to remind them on each occasion to ensure that bad habits don't develop.

Alert

Don't let your learner's apparent confidence fool you – their hazard perception skills will not be well developed, even though they think they are observing well and feel they have everything under control.

Turning/emerging left

The logbook lists turning and emerging as two separate activities. If you find this jargon confusing, the illustration should help you understand which is which. Generally it's going to be easier dealing with left turns and emerges than right because your learner won't have to cross the path of other traffic.

The ADI will teach your learner to use Mirror-Signal-Manoeuvre (MSM) at all junctions.

How you can help

Plan ahead and think of junctions where left turns can be practised. It's a good idea to find a place where your learner can drive around a left circuit or block.

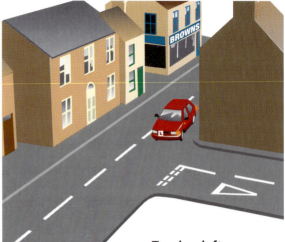

Turning left

When planning a location think

- will there be much traffic?

- can turns and emerges be practised as required?

- are there road markings to help with positioning?

- are there any difficulties such as steep slopes or poor visibility at any of the junctions?

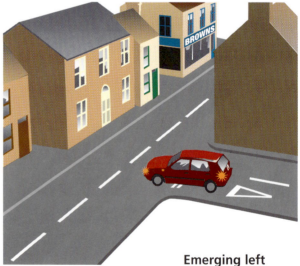

Emerging left

What to expect

Emerging left To begin with, expect your learner to

- pull up at each junction
- set the handbrake
- select first gear
- balance the clutch and accelerator

before looking to see if it's safe to pull out.

With practice this will change and the ability to slow and give way as necessary will develop. Your learner will need to recognise the difference between Give Way or Stop junctions and drive accordingly.

Alert

If your learner tries to keep the car moving when there's poor visibility, it may be driven out of the junction while their attention is focused entirely on trying to see if there's anything approaching from the right. Danger can come from

- traffic from the left, especially on narrow roads
- not steering enough, which can lead to the car being driven over to the wrong side of the road.

Turning left When turning, your learner won't normally stop and there's a lot to think about including

- mirrors
- signals
- positioning
- speed
- gear
- steering.

Alert

If your learner leaves it too late before straightening up the wheel after turning you may find the car being driven towards the pavement on the left. Make sure the speed is kept under control but don't allow your learner to let go of the wheel to let it self-centre after the turn.

Turning/emerging right

The ADI should ask your learner to practise turning and emerging right when their control skills have started to develop.

How you can help

The same considerations need to be given to choosing somewhere to practise right turns and emerges as you did for left turns. As skills develop further, you should also let your learner experience turning/emerging

- from wide and narrow roads
- in one-way streets
- at traffic lights with and without filter lanes
- across dual carriageways
- in the dark.

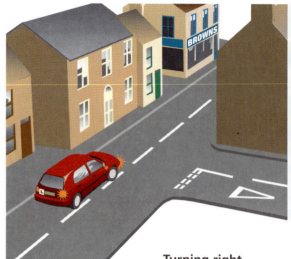

Turning right

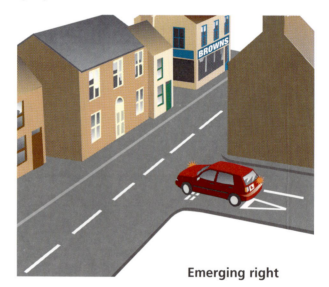

Emerging right

What to expect

Emerging right Good observation and sound judgement are called for in deciding what is a safe gap in the traffic. Expect your learner to err on the side of caution. You may find this a little frustrating at times but don't ask your learner to begin emerging on your say so. Your learner has to be able to make their own decisions and think for themselves.

Alert

Although you shouldn't decide for your learner when to emerge, you should be ready in case they make a wrong decision or don't look properly.

Turning right Expect your learner to need a little help in

* positioning the car as they approach the turn
* judging the speed of oncoming traffic.

If you need to take action to prevent a dangerous situation developing, speak firmly but don't shout.

Sometimes oncoming drivers flash their headlamps and give way to drivers waiting to turn right. Your learner needs to make their own decision whether it's safe to turn before continuing.

Alert

Expect your learner to have trouble knowing when to start turning. Too early and they cut the corner and enter on the wrong side of the road. Too late and they may hit or mount the pavement before sweeping back in an 'S' shaped arc.

Crossroads

Practising dealing with crossroads doesn't just mean turning right and left, but driving straight ahead as well. Like other junctions crossroads come in all shapes and sizes including those with

- no road markings
- road markings
- road markings and warning signs
- traffic lights.

How you can help

Take your learner through a variety of crossroads and let them practise the techniques taught by their ADI.

What to expect

When driving ahead and on the major road, your learner should be aware of the junction as they approach and pass through it.

As with right and left turns, good observation and sound judgement are called for when turning or emerging.

Expect a little exaggerated caution to start with but this should lessen to become a sensible degree of awareness.

Alert

If your learner is going ahead at a crossroad but on the minor road, they may not realise they have to give way. Road markings may be faded or difficult to see due to weather conditions or darkness and they may attempt to drive straight across as though on the major road. You might have to act quickly to prevent any danger.

Roundabouts

Many learners find roundabouts difficult to cope with. The ADI may ask for them to be practised in stages, turning left, turning right and going ahead. If that's the case you'll need to plan routes accordingly. Try to include a variety, from large multi-lane roundabouts to small and mini roundabouts.

How you can help

When you're approaching a roundabout tell your learner which direction you want them to go in plenty of time. If possible, use other instructions to help them such as 'sign posted to the town centre' or 'the third exit'. If your learner becomes disoriented, tell them in good time where their exit is to allow them time to position correctly. If they miss the exit don't worry. Direct them round again using the appropriate lane or road position and take the exit required.

You need to encourage your learner to plan their route onto, around and off the roundabout. You should try to avoid a situation where your learner is part-way around the roundabout before they start to think about which road they should be taking.

What to expect

If your learner is uncertain of the direction they are supposed to be taking expect

- incorrect signalling
- incorrect positioning
- slowness which can cause problems if there's fast moving traffic
- veering suddenly to take an exit at the last moment with no thought for other traffic.

Alert

At roundabouts rear end collisions are very common. They are often caused when a driver waiting to join a roundabout doesn't join when the driver behind expects them to. The driver behind then moves forward looking for traffic on the roundabout and not checking if the car in front has continued to move forward.

Be aware of this hazard at roundabouts.

Stationary vehicles

To a new driver there's more to dealing with parked vehicles or other obstructions than you might think.

Your learner needs to be able to identify whether they're passing one car, a line of cars or cars parked every now and then, and drive accordingly.

How you can help

You may know of some roads in your area where the road width and number of parked vehicles provide plenty of opportunity for practicing this topic. Moving past stationary vehicles will be necessary at some point in the course of most urban driving.

What to expect

You can expect some uncertainty as the learner asks themself

- should I wait or drive past?
- should I signal?
- when should I begin steering out around the car?
- have I allowed enough clearance?
- how fast should I be driving?
- are there any pedestrians trying to cross?
- is one car about to move off?
- what do I do if a car approaches once I've started to pass a line of parked cars?
- where should I be driving when there are large spaces between the parked cars?

All this questioning can lead to a late decision about how to proceed.

Alert

When faced with an oncoming vehicle your learner should be thinking, 'Do I wait or is there enough room?' Poorly developed judgement can lead to a sudden decision to try and squeeze into a space that is simply too small. Don't be caught out.

Safety of others

Your learner needs to gain experience of dealing with other road users. While other driven vehicles are obvious examples of other road users, consideration also needs to go to

- pedestrians
- cyclists
- animals and their handlers.

How you can help

It's very unlikely you're going to be able to plan to encounter any specific hazard involving another road user.

What you can do is talk to your learner about possible situations. Thinking about potential danger is a big part of developing hazard awareness.

Practising in adverse weather conditions and the dark will give your learner the chance to experience how others are affected by these conditions.

Your learner really needs to be able to 'put themselves in the other road user's shoes'. When they can do this successfully they'll be well on the way to becoming a good driver.

What to expect

In the early days, most of your learner's attention will be focused on themselves and controlling the car.

As they develop their awareness of others they may not always know how to deal with a hazard. Be ready to step in and give advice at an early stage.

Alert

There is no margin for error when dealing with vulnerable road users.

Reaction to risk

This may seem obvious but it needs stating. Before your learner can react to a risk they must perceive that a risk exists. That perception is governed by

- training. (In this situation do this.)
- experience. (I've met this before and need to do this)
- observation. (What's going on here – how should I react?)
- anticipation. (What if?)

How you can help

During practice your learner will constantly meet varying amounts of risk. While you're sat next to them, your experience in both seeing and reacting to risk should keep them safe. Where possible you can pass on the benefit of your experience.

While practising, your learner will never experience every type of risk but what you can aim for is to instil a heightened awareness of risk and how to cope with it.

What to expect

Your learner may feel they have everything under control but you may not feel that way. If the way your learner is dealing with risks makes you feel uncomfortable, something is wrong with their driving.

When a mistake has been made you'll need to tell him or her that their response to a situation or hazard was potentially dangerous. Keep calm and don't raise your voice. Learners can be defensive about their driving ability and you should take account of their feelings. However, you do need to make sure they understand the consequences of their actions.

Alert

Reaction to risk is a conscious action. If your learner gets it wrong they are either

- unaware of the risk
- showing a disregard for the safety of others.

Either way, the outcomes can be serious.

Meeting traffic

This is one area of driving practice that might put you on the edge of your seat.

Your learner has to accurately judge

- the speed and distance of oncoming traffic
- the available space
- the width of their vehicle

and answer

- wait or drive on?
- where to wait?
- what is a safe speed?
- are there any other road users to consider?

How you can help

To allow your learner to practise dealing with oncoming traffic you'll need to find places where

- the road narrows
- there are parked cars or other obstructions.

Don't just practise dealing with obstructions on your side of the road. Find places where your learner has to anticipate the actions of an approaching driver who might not give way.

What to expect

If your car is different to the ADI's your learner may take a while to get used to judging its width.

Your learner may also be indecisive. Encourage an early decision as to whether they need to wait and to plan where to stop. A late decision can lead to stopping too close to the obstruction, making it impossible to continue without first reversing.

Alert

Getting it wrong may mean your learner tries to fit into a gap that is too narrow. Don't let them go too far. There's a real danger of a collision if you do.

Crossing traffic

To clear up any misunderstanding, crossing traffic occurs when turning across the path of oncoming traffic. It has nothing to do with traffic at a pedestrian crossing, railway crossing or ferry.

How you can help

Crossing the path of approaching traffic is one of the riskier manoeuvres. The ADI will have pointed out the risks associated with turning right and explained how to manage them.

You can help by avoiding busy main road turns until confidence has developed. In addition, find places to practise that will include

- narrow roads without road markings
- roads with right-turn lane markings
- traffic lights
- box junctions.

What to expect

Learners will usually err on the side of caution. If the road is busy this might mean waiting for some time. Don't allow yourself to become frustrated because your learner won't take opportunities that seem reasonable to you. As their confidence builds, so will their ability. When waiting to turn right you may find oncoming drivers give way and invite your learner to complete turning. Before accepting this offer your learner must check for other road users, especially motorcyclists and cyclists.

Alert

Don't let your learner begin to turn when it's unsafe. The approaching driver might misinterpret the situation and react incorrectly.

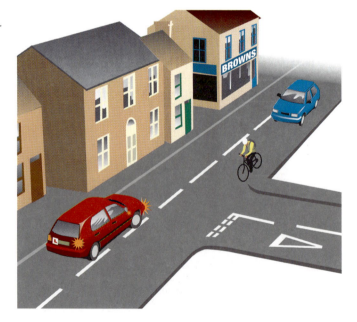

Overtaking

This refers to passing moving vehicles, not parked vehicles. It is one of the most dangerous and difficult manoeuvres for any driver. (See *The Highway Code*, rules 138–145.)

How you can help

Your learner will need to be able to overtake very slow vehicles, such as milk floats, tractors, road sweepers etc with confidence. However, don't allow your learner to overestimate their own ability or their car's performance. If they make a mistake you're there to prevent it developing into something more serious.

What to expect

There are many mistakes that may be made when overtaking, some more hazardous than others. Watch for your learner making errors born of inexperience and lack of judgement. These can include

- overtaking too slowly
- overtaking when the vehicle in front is driving at close to the speed limit
- not allowing enough room
- cutting in too soon after overtaking.

Alert

Never allow your learner to blindly follow the vehicle in front as it overtakes.

Suitable speed

Driving too fast is one of the main causes of road accidents. Driving too slowly is a different mistake and one that creates its own set of hazards. So how fast should your learner be driving? What is a suitable speed? The answer is dependent on a number of variables and getting it right takes practice.

How you can help

The more practice your learner can have of various driving situations the better they'll become at assessing the correct speed to suit different conditions.

Don't ignore rural roads where wide variations in speed can be experienced and they will have to

• plan ahead
• continually adjust their speed.

What to expect

You can expect your learner to start by driving slowly in all situations. In particular, expect very slow acceleration up through the gears, which can make emerging at junctions difficult. As experience and confidence develop, speed will increase and hazard awareness and planning ahead will then become more important. However, overconfidence and an irresponsible attitude towards risk need to be guarded against.

Alert

Make sure your learner obeys speed limits. Remember – speed limits are not targets, they are the maximum speed legally permitted. That doesn't mean it's always safe to drive up to the speed limit

It's vital that your learner understands that **they** are responsible for the consequences of their driving behaviour.

Safe distance

Driving too close to the vehicle in front is one of the most common causes of collisions. The ADI will teach your learner how to keep a safe distance from the vehicle in front, but they must then put this theory into practise when they drive.

How you can help

When your learner is following another vehicle watch how close they drive to it. Get them to tell you how they're judging a safe separation distance. See if they take into account

- road surface
- weather conditions
- speed
- visibility

and adjust the separation distance accordingly.

What to expect

Applying the two-second rule (see *The Driving Manual*) is not a complicated procedure, but you may find your learner simply forgets to apply it. This can lead to driving too close to the vehicle in front and being unaware of the risk.

Sitting next to anyone who is driving too close to the vehicle in front can be unsettling and it's important that you make your learner aware of their mistake straight away.

Alert

Your learner may never have the chance to practise driving in fog. Whether they do or not it's very important that they understand that failing to keep a safe distance when driving in fog causes many crashes each year.

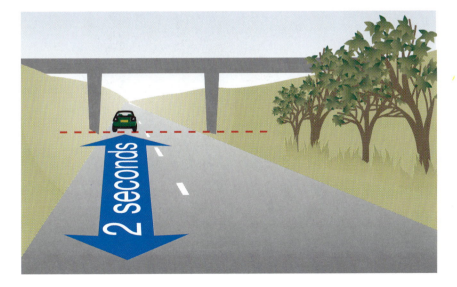

LOGBOOK TOPICS

Pedestrian crossings

There are laws governing pedestrian crossings which your learner must know and comply with. There are also several different types of pedestrian crossing (see below). Do you know them all?

How you can help

When your learner is approaching a crossing see if they can tell you what type of crossing it is and what rules apply.

Going out for a drive at school start and finish times should ensure plenty of opportunities to deal with busy crossings.

Darkness adds another aspect to safely dealing with pedestrian crossings, and practice in the dark is recommended.

What to expect

Noticing there's a crossing ahead is the first hurdle. You'll soon tell if your learner hasn't and you may need to act promptly.

Don't let your learner over-react and stop unnecessarily. This could cause a danger to following traffic.

Make certain they understand the sequence of lights at a pelican crossing and react correctly to each phase of the lights.

Alert

Pedestrians are among the most vulnerable of road users. If you have any doubts about your learner's ability to cope, give assistance until you're happy that they can cope unaided and without any risk of losing control.

Types of pedestrian crossing

Zebra crossing

Pelican crossing

Toucan crossing

Puffin crossing

Crossings controlled by an authorised person.

(See *The Highway Code*, rules 18–28 and 171–175)

DSA GUIDE TO ACCOMPANYING LEARNER DRIVERS

Dual carriageways

While a dual carriageway isn't governed by the same regulations that apply on a motorway, driving at higher speeds and in lanes on an unrestricted dual carriageway gives valuable experience both in itself and in preparation for motorway driving once the driving test has been passed.

How you can help

As well as driving in lanes along the carriageway, your learner needs to gain experience of

- using slip roads
- turning right
- overtaking
- high speed traffic.

It's also valuable to let your learner experience driving on a dual carriageway in adverse weather conditions and in the dark.

What to expect

Most learners begin by driving relatively slowly. This should not be a problem when driving along the carriageway, but joining an unrestricted dual carriageway from a slip road can call for firm acceleration. If your learner is still not confident with accelerating though the gears, wait until this skill has developed before attempting to join a dual carriageway in this manner.

When overtaking, your learner will need to judge the length of their vehicle accurately. If they don't, there's a danger of cutting in too soon as they return to the left lane.

Alert

Vehicles ahead may want to turn right through the central reserve. Don't let your learner confuse their right signal and positioning in the right lane as a sign that they are overtaking when other clues, such as brake lights or a junction sign, show they may be turning right.

Changing lanes

The ADI will teach your learner the mechanics of how to change lane using the MSM routine but it takes forward planning and timing to ensure lane changes are carried out safely and confidently.

How you can help

When you're focusing your attention on this topic, plan routes that take in the need to change lane both from left to right and right to left (for example when leaving a roundabout to complete a right turn).

You'll need to give early directions to allow your learner to take up the correct lane in good time. Encourage them to use road markings or signs to help identify the lane they need.

Don't forget there aren't always lane markings, such as around many large roundabouts, but the same rules apply to changing lane here as elsewhere.

What to expect

Learner drivers often don't think far enough ahead and this can lead to very late decisions about the need to change lane. Don't let a last-minute decision to change lane cause any danger to passing traffic or other road user.

Turning to glance into the blind spot before changing lanes can affect your learner's control of the steering. Don't allow this to endanger nearby traffic.

Alert

When driving ahead at roundabouts, your learner might change from the left lane as they enter the roundabout to the lane on their right as they go around and back to the left lane again as they leave the roundabout, without being aware they have changed lane once let alone twice. If there's traffic in the lane on the right be ready to use the steering to avoid a collision.

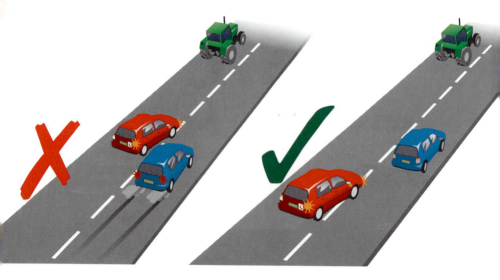

Signs/markings

It's likely that your learner will have studied for their theory test and learnt the meanings, of all the road signs and markings in *The Highway Code*. Putting that knowledge into practise might not be as easy as you'd imagine.

The learner driver has to first

* see the sign or markings and realise it affects them

and secondly

* follow the direction given by the sign or marking.

How you can help

The greater the variety of signs and markings your learner has to deal with while practising the better.

Signs giving

* orders
* positive instructions

need particular attention. Making a mistake on one of these signs might mean committing an offence under the Road Traffic Act.

What to expect

You can expect your learner to have so much to think about that they fail to notice some traffic signs and road markings. This can be anything from failing to notice a change of speed limit to trying to drive past a 'No Entry' sign.

Practising at night or in bad weather will make this more likely, especially where road markings are faded or worn.

Alert

Remember that, as the accompanying driver, you are responsible for your learner and may be prosecuted if you allow any offence to be committed.

Progress

While your learner must never drive beyond their ability or the speed limit, they will need to reach a level where they can drive on all roads without hindering the flow of traffic.

How you can help

If you have a timid driver remember that timid people take a long time to feel confident with making progress.

If you think your learner is not improving very quickly, don't be negative or critical – a timid driver needs encouragement not criticism. Learning to drive is a lengthy process and you just need to allow more time and more practice.

What to expect

Accompanying a learner who drives slowly and takes a long time to move off or emerge at junctions can become very frustrating. Don't let your learner drive the car if you're in a hurry to get somewhere since this will only make you feel worse.

You need to be

- patient
- tolerant
- understanding.

If you're critical and negative, what sort of message do you think this gives your learner about correct driver behaviour towards other road users?

Alert

Your learner must understand that making progress does not mean driving up to the speed limit without consideration for road and traffic conditions.

Emergency stop

Practising stopping the car as if there was an emergency provides valuable experience in

- reacting quickly
- reacting correctly
- controlling the car under emergency conditions.

Training for an emergency should help your learner to cope if an emergency situation ever arises.

How you can help

To practise stopping in an emergency you need to find somewhere

- with very little traffic
- where screeching tyres won't cause a nuisance
- with a good road surface.

Agree with your learner the signal to give and begin practising at low speeds. Only progress to practising at higher speeds when your learner has the control skills to cope.

What to expect

The ADI will have given instruction in use of the controls. If your vehicle has an anti-lock braking system fitted there may be special instructions on how to achieve maximum braking.

Be prepared for your learner using excessive force when applying the brakes. This may cause

- skidding accompanied by loud screeching and smoke from the tyres
- a severe jolt which could cause injury to your back or neck.

Before you give any signal to stop make sure you're braced and prepared for sudden rapid deceleration.

Alert

Make certain you look around before giving any signal to stop. Relying on your additional interior mirror to tell you what's behind isn't enough.

Turn in the road

Turning the car around in the road should not be looked upon as an exercise to be practised just for the driving test. The skills needed to carry out this exercise will be needed every time your learner has to manoeuvre their car in a confined space.

How you can help

You may wish to familiarise yourself with the technique your learner will have been taught by their ADI. This is explained in detail in *The Driving Manual*.

When looking for a place to practise the exercise consider

- the road width
- the amount of traffic you can expect
- visibility
- local residents.

Be courteous to other road users while your learner is practising. Be prepared to find somewhere else if the place you have chosen turns out to be less suitable than you first thought.

What to expect

Your learner may

- struggle with the controls
- be unable to judge the car's length
- fail to notice other road users.

Some learners can take a long time to remember the techniques they've been taught. Panic can set in and they can become disoriented when half way through the exercise.

You'll need to be supportive and offer encouragement not criticism if it's all taking longer than you thought it would.

Alert

A sudden loss of control when turning can result in surging forward or backwards over the kerb, onto the pavement and colliding with whatever is in the way. You'll need to act promptly if your learner loses control in this manner.

Reversing to the left and right

To many learners, reversing accurately is the most difficult part of learning to drive. The statistics also show this as a key reason for learners failing the driving test. If your learner finds reversing difficult you can expect to spend a lot of time practising this skill.

How you can help

It is easier to begin by practising reversing into a junction on the left rather than the right. The techniques for reversing both to the left and right are described in *The Driving Manual.*

Look for a place to practise where

- there's good visibility
- the road is level
- you don't expect much traffic
- you won't annoy local residents.

A crossroads or staggered junction is **not** a suitable location to practise reversing. Don't just use one location but find a variety of junctions for practice sessions.

What to expect

Reversing doesn't come easily to many learners and if your learner becomes despondent then move on to another topic and return to reversing practice another day.

Practising on an uphill slope before skills have developed is likely to cause wear on the clutch and noise as the engine is excessively revved.

Alert

Modern cars have an exterior mirror fitted on both sides of the car. If these mirrors are used for reversing

- there is no view directly behind the car
- the driver may focus solely on the detail seen in the mirror and fail to see other road users or obstructions
- they are not set for rear observation when driving.

Reversing a car using only mirrors, rather than turning and looking behind, is not recommended.

Reverse park

This is an exercise your learner may be asked to demonstrate during their driving test. It's also an important skill your learner is going to need once they've passed their driving test.

How you can help

When practising this skill your learner will inevitably cause a temporary obstruction to any traffic flow. For this reason a quiet location is essential.

To begin with, your learner may find it easier to practise parking behind one single car rather than between two cars. *The Driving Manual* explains the recommended procedure for this manoeuvre.

While your learner's car control skills are developing you can help by being their eyes and ears, watching out for other road users. As their car control develops, you can let them become responsible for the safety aspects themselves.

What to expect

When your learner sets about reverse parking you can expect them to have trouble judging where to pull up in readiness to reverse into the space. This may result in pulling up

- too close alongside the parked car
- too far past the parked car
- not far enough forward past the parking space.

You may find some car owners are not happy for learners to use their car to practise around and may move their vehicle.

Alert

You must ensure your learner doesn't hit any other vehicle while they're practising this manoeuvre. You are responsible.

Use of car parks

Reversing into a parking space in a car park is another reversing manoeuvre your learner may be asked to perform during their driving test. It's also a very necessary skill for modern day driving.

Your learner should be able to reverse into a parking space and position the car neatly in the parking bay.

How you can help

You'll need to find a car park where your learner can practise this manoeuvre. Avoid busy car parks and peak times of day.

Try to find a parking bay that has an empty bay on either side. This will allow a greater margin for inaccurate steering.

As with other reverse manoeuvres, don't allow your learner to rely on the car's mirrors while reversing.

What to expect

To reverse neatly into a parking bay calls for

- accuracy
- control
- judgement.

Your learner may be weak on any or all of these skills. If they misjudge the car's length they may attempt to reverse back beyond the edge of the bay. This could result in colliding with the car park wall or barrier and damaging your car.

Alert

In multi-storey car parks there are many support pillars which can be difficult to see when reversing. Colliding with one of these can cause extensive bodywork damage to your car.

PART THREE FURTHER INFORMATION

This part gives further information that you may find useful.

The topics include

- Approved Driving Instructors
- The driving test
- Pass Plus
- Useful addresses

Approved Driving Instructors

An ADI is approved by DSA to teach learner drivers for payment.

DSA is responsible for maintaining and checking the standards of all ADIs, who must

- have held a full driving licence for at least four years
- pass a written exam lasting 90 minutes
- pass a strict driving test
- reach and keep up a high standard of instruction. ADIs are regularly checked by a supervising examiner from DSA
- be registered with DSA
- display an ADI identification certificate on the windscreen of the tuition vehicle.

A learner must use an ADI or a trainee-licence holder if they want to pay someone to teach the practical skills of driving.

Some trainee driving instructors are granted a trainee licence so that they can gain teaching experience before their qualifying examination. This licence is a pink identification certificate which must be displayed on the windscreen of the tuition vehicle.

How to choose an ADI

Your learner may ask you to help choose an ADI. You may have no experience or knowledge of local driving instructors and, rather than base your advice simply on cost, you should consider

- asking friends and relatives
- choosing an instructor
    - who has a good reputation
    - is reliable and punctual
    - whose car suits your learner
- referring to the leaflet 'Learning to drive' which is sent out with all provisional driving licences. This explains ADI grading.

Voluntary Code of Practice

A voluntary Code of Practice has been agreed within the driving instruction industry. The code covers the following matters in relation to ADIs

- their level of qualification
- the personal conduct expected from them when giving tuition
- the professional conduct of their business
- the acceptability of their advertising
- their method of dealing with complaints.

For further information or advice telephone DSA – see 'Useful addresses' for the number.

The driving test

You'll probably be anxious to know when your learner will be ready to pass their driving test.

The ADI will be able to tell you, but as a guide use this checklist. If you can tick all the boxes your learner should be ready to take their driving test.

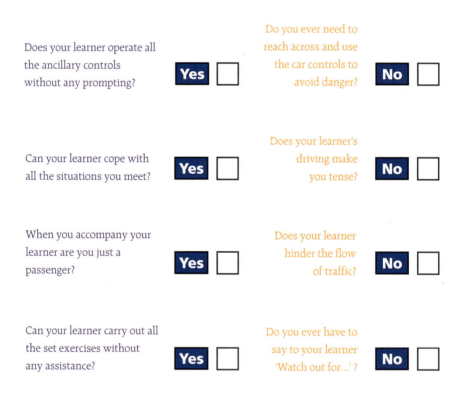

Does your learner operate all the ancillary controls without any prompting? **Yes** ☐

Do you ever need to reach across and use the car controls to avoid danger? **No** ☐

Can your learner cope with all the situations you meet? **Yes** ☐

Does your learner's driving make you tense? **No** ☐

When you accompany your learner are you just a passenger? **Yes** ☐

Does your learner hinder the flow of traffic? **No** ☐

Can your learner carry out all the set exercises without any assistance? **Yes** ☐

Do you ever have to say to your learner 'Watch out for...' ? **No** ☐

The course has to be paid for but, if completed successfully, discounts are available on car insurance from the companies taking part in the scheme. The precise saving will depend on the company.

Fees for the Pass Plus course will vary depending on the instructor or driving school.

Taking part in the scheme shows a commitment to wanting to be a safe, skilful and responsible driver.

Pass Plus

Pass Plus is a training scheme linked to insurance discounts that can benefit the **newly qualified** driver by

- saving money on car insurance
- showing a positive driving style which is both enjoyable and safe
- helping to build quality driving experience.

The Pass Plus scheme has been developed by the Department of the Environment, Transport and the Regions with the help of insurers and the driving instruction industry. The scheme has been developed to

- improve skills in areas that learners may have little experience
- reduce the risk of being involved in a road accident.

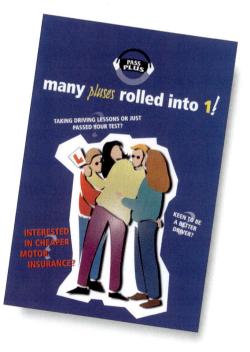

The aim of the Pass Plus scheme

The Pass Plus scheme will

- speed up the process of gaining good driving experience
- teach positive driving skills.

Throughout the course the newly qualified driver will be driving with two key factors in mind.

Attitude

- responsibility for their actions
- care and consideration for others.

Skills

- observation
- assessing what they see
- making decisions
- taking the right action.

Your instructor will explain why they are the key to a **positive driving** style.

Useful addresses

DSA test enquiries and booking centre

DSA
PO Box 280
Newcastle-upon-Tyne
NE99 1FP

Tel: 0870 01 01 372
Welsh Speakers: 0870 01 00 372
Minicom: 0870 01 07 372
Fax: 0870 01 02 372

DSA Head Office

Stanley House
56 Talbot Street
Nottingham NG1 5GU

Tel: 0115 901 2500
Fax: 0115 901 2940
Website: www.driving-tests.co.uk

Approved Driving Instructors' National Joint Council

The Secretary
41 Edinburgh Road
Cambridge CB4 1QR

Tel & Fax: 01223 359079

DETR Mobility Advice and Vehicle Information Service (MAVIS)

'O' Wing
McAdam Avenue
Old Wokingham Rd
Crowthorne
Berkshire RG45 6XD

Tel: 01344 661000
Fax: 01344 661066
Website: www.mobility-unit.detr.gov.uk/

Driver and Vehicle Licencing Agency (DVLA)

Customer Enquiry Unit
Swansea SA6 7JL

Tel: 0179 277 2151
Website: www.open.gov.uk/dvla/welcome.htm

Driving Instructors' Association

Safety House
Beddington Farm Road
Croydon CR0 4XZ

Tel: 0181 665 5151
Fax: 0181 665 5565
Website: www.driving.org

Motor Schools Association of Great Britain Ltd

182A Heaton Moor Road
Stockport
Cheshire SK4 4DU

Tel: 0161 443 1611
Fax: 0161 443 1699
Website: www.msagb.co.uk

The Association of Driving Instructors' Business Club

3 Greenacre Close
Wyke
Bradford
West Yorkshire BD12 9DQ

Tel: 01274 672850

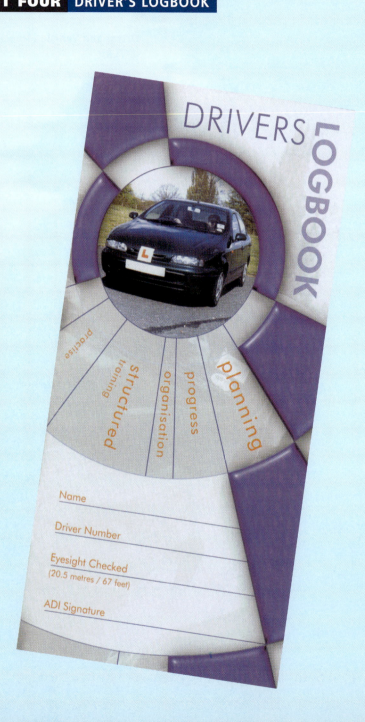

DRIVERS LOGBOOK

practise

structured
training

organisation

progress

planning

Name

Driver Number

Eyesight Checked
(20.5 metres / 67 feet)

ADI Signature

Lesson record

Instructor's comments

Your instructor will record here a brief description of how your lesson went and what you need to concentrate on in your next lesson.

Private practice needed

Your instructor will give you advice on this and will note here what you should practise before your next lesson. This may include day / night / town / country driving.

Pupil's comments

You should think carefully about your lesson and record here what you think the good points were and what your comments are, if you have any.

---

example

Date _1/5/99_ Duration _45_ Mileage _15_

Instructor's Initials _AHA_

Comments _Trevor needs to make sure he takes effective observation when reversing. Introduced dual carriageways_

Private Practice Needed _Reverse-parking observation_

Pupil's Comments _I felt a bit unsure of the higher speed on the A41 but enjoyed it_

1

Date............................Duration............................Mileage............................

Instructor's Initials............................

Comments............................

....

....

....

Private Practice Needed............................

....

Pupil's Comments............................

....

....

2

Date............................Duration............................Mileage............................

Instructor's Initials............................

Comments............................

....

....

....

Private Practice Needed............................

....

Pupil's Comments............................

....

....

3

Date................................Duration............................Mileage..

Instructor's Initials..

Comments...

....

....

....

Private Practice Needed..

....

Pupil's Comments..

....

....

4

Date................................Duration............................Mileage..

Instructor's Initials..

Comments...

....

....

....

Private Practice Needed..

....

Pupil's Comments..

....

....

5

Date................................Duration......................Mileage..

Instructor's Initials...

Comments..

....

....

....

Private Practice Needed..

....

Pupil's Comments..

....

....

6

Date................................Duration......................Mileage..

Instructor's Initials...

Comments..

....

....

....

Private Practice Needed..

....

Pupil's Comments..

....

....

7

Date................................Duration....................Mileage...

Instructor's Initials..

Comments...

....

....

....

Private Practice Needed...

....

Pupil's Comments...

....

....

8

Date................................Duration....................Mileage...

Instructor's Initials..

Comments...

....

....

....

Private Practice Needed...

....

Pupil's Comments...

....

....

9

Date........................Duration.....................Mileage...............................

Instructor's Initials..

Comments...

Private Practice Needed..

Pupil's Comments..

10

Date........................Duration.....................Mileage...............................

Instructor's Initials..

Comments...

Private Practice Needed..

Pupil's Comments..

11

Date................................Duration...........................Mileage...

Instructor's Initials...

Comments..

....

....

....

Private Practice Needed...

....

Pupil's Comments...

....

....

12

Date................................Duration...........................Mileage...

Instructor's Initials...

Comments..

....

....

....

Private Practice Needed...

....

Pupil's Comments...

....

....

13

Date........................Duration....................Mileage..............................

Instructor's Initials...

Comments...

....

....

....

Private Practice Needed..

....

Pupil's Comments...

....

....

14

Date........................Duration....................Mileage..............................

Instructor's Initials...

Comments...

....

....

....

Private Practice Needed..

....

Pupil's Comments...

....

....

15

Date.................................Duration..................Mileage................................

Instructor's Initials..

Comments...

Private Practice Needed...

Pupil's Comments...

16

Date.................................Duration..................Mileage................................

Instructor's Initials..

Comments...

Private Practice Needed...

Pupil's Comments...

17

Date.................................Duration.................Mileage.................................

Instructor's Initials...

Comments...

....

....

....

Private Practice Needed..

....

Pupil's Comments..

....

....

18

Date.................................Duration.................Mileage.................................

Instructor's Initials...

Comments...

....

....

....

Private Practice Needed..

....

Pupil's Comments..

....

....

19

Date......................Duration......................Mileage......................

Instructor's Initials......................

Comments......................

....

....

....

Private Practice Needed......................

....

Pupil's Comments......................

....

....

20

Date......................Duration......................Mileage......................

Instructor's Initials......................

Comments......................

....

....

....

Private Practice Needed......................

....

Pupil's Comments......................

....

....

21

Date............................Duration............................Mileage............................

Instructor's Initials............................

Comments............................

....

....

....

Private Practice Needed............................

....

Pupil's Comments............................

....

....

22

Date............................Duration............................Mileage............................

Instructor's Initials............................

Comments............................

....

....

....

Private Practice Needed............................

....

Pupil's Comments............................

....

....

23

Date................Duration................Mileage................

Instructor's Initials................
Comments................

Private Practice Needed................

Pupil's Comments................

24

Date................Duration................Mileage................

Instructor's Initials................
Comments................

Private Practice Needed................

Pupil's Comments................

25

Date...................................Duration.....................Mileage.......................................

Instructor's Initials..

Comments...

....

....

....

Private Practice Needed..

....

Pupil's Comments...

....

....

26

Date...................................Duration.....................Mileage.......................................

Instructor's Initials..

Comments...

....

....

....

Private Practice Needed..

....

Pupil's Comments...

....

....

27

Date........................Duration....................Mileage..

Instructor's Initials...

Comments..

....

....

....

Private Practice Needed..

....

Pupil's Comments..

....

....

28

Date........................Duration....................Mileage..

Instructor's Initials...

Comments..

....

....

....

Private Practice Needed..

....

Pupil's Comments..

....

....

29

Date.................Duration.................Mileage.................

Instructor's Initials.................
Comments.................

Private Practice Needed.................

Pupil's Comments.................

30

Date.................Duration.................Mileage.................

Instructor's Initials.................
Comments.................

Private Practice Needed.................

Pupil's Comments.................

31

Date................................Duration.................Mileage...

Instructor's Initials..

Comments..

....

....

Private Practice Needed..

Pupil's Comments...

....

32

Date................................Duration.................Mileage...

Instructor's Initials..

Comments..

....

....

Private Practice Needed..

Pupil's Comments...

....

Progress record

This section allows your instructor to record your progress. The following list of topics is based on the officially recommended syllabus for learning to drive. The syllabus is explained fully in *The Driving Test*, one of the DSA Official Driving series of books.

You can see your progress as your instructor completes this chart.

1 Introduced	2 Under full instruction	3 Prompted	4 Seldom prompted	5 Independent

Lesson	1 2 3 4 5 6 7 8 9 10 11 12 13 14 15 16 17 18 19 20 21 22 23 24 25 26 27 28 29 30 31 32

Topics

Highway Code	
Vehicle Checks	
Ancillary Controls	
Starting the Engine	
Use of Car Controls	

Lesson	1	2	3	4	5	6	7	8	9	10	11	12	13	14	15	16	17	18	19	20	21	22	23	24	25	26	27	28	29	30	31	32
Moving Off																																
On the Level																																
Uphill																																
Downhill																																
At an Angle																																
Position on the Road																																
Proper Observations																																
Blind Spots																																
Forward Observations																																
Use of Mirrors																																
Turning Left																																
Emerging Left																																

1 Introduced 2 Under full instruction 3 Prompted 4 Seldom prompted 5 Independent

Lesson	1	2	3	4	5	6	7	8	9	10	11	12	13	14	15	16	17	18	19	20	21	22	23	24	25	26	27	28	29	30	31	32
Turning Right																																
Emerging Right																																
Crossroads																																
Roundabouts																																
Stationary Vehicles																																
Safety of Others																																
Reaction to Risks																																
Meeting Traffic																																
Crossing Traffic																																
Overtaking																																
Suitable Speed																																

Lesson	1	2	3	4	5	6	7	8	9	10	11	12	13	14	15	16	17	18	19	20	21	22	23	24	25	26	27	28	29	30	31	32
Safe Distance																																
Pedestrian Crossings																																
Dual Carriageways																																
Changing Lanes																																
Signs / Markings																																
Progress																																
Town																																
Country																																
Emergency Stop																																
Turn in the Road																																
Reverse Left																																
Reverse Right																																

Lesson	1 Introduced	2 Under full instruction	3 Prompted	4 Seldom prompted	5 Independent

Column numbers: 1 2 3 4 5 6 7 8 9 10 11 12 13 14 15 16 17 18 19 20 21 22 23 24 25 26 27 28 29 30 31 32

Reverse Park

Use of Car Parks

Environmental Issues *

Railway Crossings *

Adverse Weather *

Night Driving *

You must know about motorway rules, regulations and driving techniques before you take your test. After passing your test, lessons are recommended with an ADI before driving unsupervised on motorways.

Motorways

*Discuss these topics with your ADI.

Private Practice

Take careful note of the advice your instructor has given you in your lessons. Write here brief details of any driving you have done between lessons and the things you have practised. Also make a note of any worries you may have so that you can talk about them to your instructor. Use as much space as you need to make your comments.

Private Practice Record										
Date	Night	Day	Town	Country	Wet	Dry	Dual	Comments	Time	Miles

Private Practice Record

Date	Night	Day	Town	Country	Wet	Dry	Dual	Comments	Time	Miles

Private Practice Record

Date	Night	Day	Town	Country	Wet	Dry	Dual	Comments	Time	Miles

Private Practice Record

Date	Night	Day	Town	Country	Wet	Dry	Dual	Comments	Time	Miles

Private Practice Record

Date	Night	Day	Town	Country	Wet	Dry	Dual	Comments	Time	Miles

Private Practice Record

Date	Night	Day	Town	Country	Wet	Dry	Dual	Comments	Time	Miles

Private Practice Record

Date	Night	Day	Town	Country	Wet	Dry	Dual	Comments	Time	Miles

The Theory Test

Normally, you will have to take and pass a theory test before your application for the practical test is accepted.

You don't have to pass your theory test before you start your lessons; indeed, you are strongly advised to study both theory and practical skills at the same time.

During your practical lessons, your instructor will ask you questions on the Highway Code, even if you have taken and passed your theory test.

The topics covered are listed here. As you study, tick the first box when you think you have covered each topic fully. Your instructor will then test you on the topic before ticking the second box.

Alertness ☐ ☐

- Observation
- Anticipation
- Concentration
- Awareness
- Distraction

Attitude ☐ ☐

- Consideration
- Positioning
- Courtesy
- Priority

Safety and Your Vehicle ☐ ☐

- Fault Detection
- Defects
- Safety Equipment
- Emissions
- Noise

Safety Margins ☐ ☐

- Stopping Distances
- Road Surfaces
- Skidding
- Weather Conditions

Vehicle Handling ☐ ☐

- Weather Conditions
- Road Conditions
- Time of Day
- Speed
- Traffic Calming

Vulnerable Road Users ☐ ☐

- People with Disabilities
- Pedestrians
- Children
- Cyclists
- Elderly
- Motorcyclists
- Horseriders

Other Types of Vehicle ☐ ☐

- Motorcycles
- Lorries
- Buses

Motorway Rules ☐ ☐

- Speed Limits
- Lane Discipline
- Stopping
- Lighting
- Parking

Rules of the Road ☐ ☐

- Speed Limits
- Parking
- Lighting

Road and Traffic Signs ☐ ☐

- Road Signs
- Speed Limits
- Road Markings
- Regulations

Hazard Awareness ☐ ☐

- Anticipation
- Hazard Awareness
- Attention
- Speed and Distance
- Reaction Time
- Alcohol and Drugs
- Tiredness

Accidents ☐ ☐

- First Aid
- Warning Devices
- Reporting Procedures
- Safety Regulations

Documents ☐ ☐

- Licence
- Insurance
- MOT

Vehicle Loading ☐ ☐

- Stability
- Loading Regulations

Test record

Date of Theory Test pass ....

Declaration of syllabus covered

I certify that..
has received instruction in all the topics on pages
22–27 of this logbook and is fully prepared to take
the test.

Signed ....

Name...

ADI No...

Date...

Note: Although your ADI feels that you are ready to take your test, this is not
a guarantee that you will pass.

Declaration of syllabus covered

I certify that..
has received instruction in all the topics on pages
20–25 of this logbook and is fully prepared to take
the test.

Signed ....

Name...

ADI No...

Date...

Note: Although your ADI feels that you are ready to take your test, this is not
a guarantee that you will pass.

Date of Practical Test pass...

Date Pass Plus completed..

If you pass your Driving Test

Well done. Passing your driving test is the first stage in a life time of **learning by experience**. Look at the driving test report you have been given and discuss it with your instructor. This is given to you to help you overcome any weaknesses in your driving. As you gain experience in driving you should be aiming to improve your driving skills. After passing your driving test, consider taking Pass Plus and at some future stage an advanced driving test.

If you fail your Driving Test

Your driving has not reached the standard required. You will have made mistakes which could have caused danger on the road.

Your examiner will help you by

- giving you a driving test report form. This will show all the faults marked during the test
- explain briefly why you didn't pass.

You should listen to your examiner carefully who will be able to help you by pointing out the aspects of your driving you need to improve. Study the Driving Test Report and refer to the relevant sections in this booklet.

Show your copy of the report to your ADI, who will advise and help you to correct the faults.

Listen to your ADI's advice carefully as you will need to cover some of the syllabus again and get as much practice as you can.

Printed in the United Kingdom for The Stationery Office TJ000778 03/00 C100 63789

The Stationery Office publishes a wide range of essential titles for new and established motorists

The Highway Code

New expanded edition

Completely revised to include new legislation, with greater emphasis on safe driving and special sections on vulnerable road users such as horse riders, cyclists and the elderly. This new expanded edition has a useful index plus advice on rules dealing with driver fatigue and recommendations on the use of mobile phones.

0 11 551977 7   £1.49

Know Your Traffic Signs

The most comprehensive explanation of road signs available

Illustrating and explaining the vast majority of traffic signals, signs and road markings that any road user is likely to encounter. Exceptional value for money.

ISBN 0 11 551612 3   £2.50

The Official Theory Test for Car Drivers and Motorcyclists

New touchscreen edition

This best-selling title is the only official theory test publication and is written and compiled by the DSA to help you pass the theory test. Covering all aspects of the test, it is the most comprehensive guide available and contains the very latest information as well as the DSA's question bank of around 1,000 theory test questions in an easy-to-use format.

0 11 552202 6   £11.99

Test Yourself Papers for the Driving Theory Test

Five practice papers for the theory test

Questions taken from the DSA's official theory test question bank with the correct answers supplied for further reference and revision.

ISBN 0 11 551984 X   £4.99 (INCL VAT)

The Official Driving Test

The practical driving test

Fully illustrated and written in a clear and easy-to-understand style. Fully updated with the officially recommended syllabus for learning to drive.

0 11 552190 9   £6.99

The Official Driving Manual

The official guide to safer driving

The essential reference manual for all motorists and instructors, covering subjects as diverse as defensive driving, bends and junctions, manoeuvring, towing and European driving, plus legal information.

0 11 552191 7   £12.99

For further details visit the Driving & Transport portal of our website:

www.itsofficial.net

Order Form

Please send me the following titles:

Title	ISBN	Price	Quantity
The Highway Code	0 11 551977 7	£1.49	....
Know Your Traffic Signs	0 11 551612 3	£2.50	....
The Official Theory Test for Car Drivers and Motorcyclists	0 11 552202 6	£11.99	....
Test Yourself Papers for the Driving Theory Test	0 11 551984 X	£4.99 (incl VAT)	....
The Driving Test	0 11 552190 9	£6.99	....
The Driving Manual	0 11 552191 7	£12.99	....
Handling charge per order:		£2.50	

(Or £2.94 if your order includes Test Papers)

Total enclosed: £.................

PLEASE COMPLETE IN BLOCK CAPITALS

Name...

Address ....

....

....

.... Postcode............................... AHQ

☐ I enclose a cheque for £.................... payable to: *'The Stationery Office'*

☐ Please charge to my account with The Stationery Office, No:

....

☐ Please debit my Mastercard/Visa/Amex/Diners/Connect Card Account No.

Signature.. Expiry date ....

The Stationery Office

DSA DRIVING STANDARDS AGENCY
SAFE DRIVING FOR LIFE